Almanac of Reckoning

poems by

Sandra Salinas Newton

Finishing Line Press
Georgetown, Kentucky

Almanac of Reckoning

ACKNOWLEDGMENTS

"At A Party of Mourning Doves in Austin, Texas" in *Connecticut River Review*
"Cutting Back" in *OPEN: Journal of Arts and Letters*
"Dawn Yard in March" in *Inverted Syntax*
"Fountain" in *Midwest Quarterly*
"Lady Spring" in *The MacGuffin*
"Morning" in *Etched Onyx*
"Our Place" in *boats against the current*
"Permanence" in *The Poetry Box and in Slab*
"Spirit" in *Hyacinth Review*
"Waking" in *Brushfire*
"Warnings" in *OPEN: Journal of Arts and Letters*
"Winter Roses" in Cerasus, reprinted as "Against the Grain" in *Multiplicity*
"Ylang-Ylang" in *Etched Onyx*
What Is Not There" in *Vita Brevis*

Publisher: Leah Huete de Maines
Editor: Christen Kincaid
Cover Art: Sandra S. Newton
Author Photo: Sandra S. Newton
Cover Design: Elizabeth Maines McCleavy

Order online: www.finishinglinepress.com
also available on amazon.com

Author inquiries and mail orders:
Finishing Line Press
PO Box 1626
Georgetown, Kentucky 40324
USA

Contents

Winter

The wind carries the smell of snow, that icy odor of hard blue
Stinging the nostrils and trembling the cheeks,
The air a friendless heap of cold growing heavy
As the day begins its daily surrender to night.

We hear the start of settling all around us:
Birds quibbling over places on a leaf-lorn branch,
Simple sand being sifted against a careless night wind,
And the cautious possum digging out,
Watching for starlight to guide him to an evening's meal.

Dreams and nightmares come crawling forth
 In such a dusk so filled with the menace of snow
Against which we huddle and cluster
Making warm knots of ourselves with arms and legs
And blow into our hands the warm puffs of air
To chase the taste of snow away.

Winter should be
Our time for warm memories.

Quercus Virginiana (Southern Live Oak)

The oak in the front yard was attacked by
The night storm that hunkered down over us
This past winter. She resisted,
Crying with the pitiful moans of
Helplessness—a creaking sound
That eventually cracked like thunder,
Then whooshed as her arm fell broken
To her side.

When I went out in the crisp morning
Catching my breath with the sharp cold,
I saw her standing
Forlorn and silent now
While contemplating the slender
Acorns she will no longer drop,
Rolling carefree into a summer's gutter.

And after I dragged her broken limb
To one side, I looked up to see
She could only shield me partially now
From the angry gods in the sky.

Ice Storm

The ice has brought the branches
To their knees
Bowing heavily to the cold
That is too cruel
For snow.

No warmth allowed:
Crepe myrtle set in hard glass
And palms drooping with exhaustion
Held captive
In frozen chains.

On unyielding boughs
The blue jays skip nervously
Searching the stiff ground below
For bits of food—
Broken grain, corn, millet, and grit—
To ease their chill
Another day.

I am warm inside
With comforts at hand
Yet the ice stands firm at my door
Ready, I know, to grip my heart.

Winter Roses

For a city girl, unaccustomed to greenery
Except in a salad or along the edges of my eyes
As the taxi rolls past Central Park
I am surprised each winter by a rose bush
That refuses to die and is even brash enough
To wait until the onset of winter to bloom.

Long exiled to Texas by dint of illness
Fatigue and marital circumstance
I watched my husband plant seeds and tiny plantlets
Pots of green and hues of countrysides
As if he knew that he would die and they
Would outlive him like careless children
Left with me the ignorant step-mother
Yearning for asphalt and steel and sooty air.

But these winter roses scraggly and malnourished
Screaming their pinkness because red demands
A rich blood which they do not have
Still breathe and thrive in the bracing cool air
And learn to live against the grain
Of expectation.

Cutting Back

Miguel cut back all the branches
Of things that died recently.
First we had a freeze and then in
Recovery a raging wind,
Murderers rampaging through
Texas like outlaws of the old days.
My loquat stood tall
But died in its roots
The thick, oily leaves turning brown
And stiff
Dead where they lay.
The banana, which every year
Grew quiet in the soil until April
And then pushed joyfully out
To sunbathe,
This year died under the ice
A poor drowned and careless child.
And the hedges that shielded
My life from the prying outside
Standing guard against my window
Simply froze in place
Skeletons of Spring that needed
Disassembly.
All that is left is the fig tree
Usually green and boasting fertility by now
Stark, naked, gnarled
An old and undesired woman
That the grackles and jays now avoid
Still I wait
And hope
Desperate for buds to appear
For your pale green fruit to burst
Dripping with a sweet promise
That nothing has changed
All will be well.

Warnings

Yesterday at the shop I chose plants
To replace what winter had pillaged
Leaving a moist fecundity behind.

And so, imperiously, I said to the gardener,
"This one and that,
And perhaps that other as well."

I had looked only for appearance
To fill some empty spaces.

And then the pattern and the meaning emerged
Fixed upon me by a knowing eye:

Whale's tongue agave was exotic beauty
The tough earth and rolling sea in one;

Tropical banana was fragility
A tall, leafless stalk trembling defiantly;

And oleander was cautious destiny
Small pink flowers like nipples
Attracting the careless heart.

Our days are only stale memories
Begging water from the cloudless sky
And warmth from rocky earth:
Destiny of a fragile, exotic beauty.

Lady Spring

It will be a vicious spring   I am sure of it
      The wife of bitter winter Who turned cold in bed
And refused her overtures   Of mild and gentle rain
    She is angry now and will not forgive.

Instead of sweet showers
                      Scented with early rose
                      Dwarf iris and snowdrop
She will rage in torrents
     To drown all that dare   To bring pleasure
     To the softening earth   To the baby buds
And laugh to hear their sinking cries.

She aches to feel the growing of summer
In her womb
        Remembrance of winter's caresses
        In his clouded mild nights
She waits to hear his footsteps drawing close
To her bed
        Because even his cold embrace
        Is better than an empty space
Beside her   Under the uncertain moon.

Dawn Yard in March

Five a.m. unrisen sun
Illuminates the yard
In cloud-gray light.

A possum
Freak child of rat and raccoon
Nibbles at yesterday's
Birdseed and tostada shards
Eyes black and endless
That swallow the light.

Early jays trampoline
Branch to branch
Flapping dark wings
To complain their hungry bellies.

Two feral cats
Poised in far corners
Await meals hastily
Spooned into dishes and
Dropped at the door.

I step back inside
Intruder in my own yard
The natural world
In perfect tolerance without me.

Garden Lesson

The jay dips into the fountain
And when she lifts her head
The sun twinkles like a star
Off the point of her beak:

A knowing wink to the garden
That warmth and water are
Salvation from despair.

                The earth is where
We bury our grievance of loss,
                The air where we rejoice
At a drop of water swallowed

By the jay who
Understands redemption.

La Pluie

I am held captive today although
You had been so gentle and caressing before;
But today you flexed muscle and iron will
To keep me indoors.

Paris, you thought, needed a cleaning of sorts:
Scrubbing raw to dispel the filth
Of cold Spring days that kill the new buds
And keep the leaves shivering brown and orange.

So, rain.
Not the showers whose each drop
Fondles my cheek
Or tickles the tips of my ears.

Real rain:
Sheets of water carried on the wind
Piercing tattoos on the skin
Chilling the roots of hair
And dampening the toes.

I had hoped to walk today, to
Wander the Luxembourg Gardens,
But could only pace the floors
Of my empty apartment
And listen to you chattering
As you slid down the rooftop tiles
And my laptop keys punched out
A struggling song.

At A Party of Mourning Doves in Austin, Texas

A loft of doves rushes down to peck
At the seeds and broken tostadas thrown
Into the winter yard.

They clump together
                            like nervous girls
at a quinceañera
Bodies hot and trembling
With perilous anticipation.

The doves cannot stand still
But stamp their lightly taloned feet
And sing soft melodies to each other
While gulping down the charity
In frosty air.

Without strategy or tactic
They feed and worry;
                            one or two duennas
                            lookouts
                            for the murdering cats
                            who prowl this yard.

When the feast is over
Only one will have fallen
Caught in claws
Devoured, not unlike
                            the innocent beauty
                            who succumbs
                            astonished
                            to the fastest boy
While the rest
Complacent and stuffed
Fly home
Completely unaware.

Les Pigeons

I think the pigeons own Paris,
Strutting with studied arrogance, unafraid

Of human feet. They tease and taunt us,
Daring to walk among us as if we were chattel.

But, note they own the streets and the skies,
Their arms carry them upward,

And ours swing uselessly astride.

Sapling

I am glad now to have found the tears
That so long ago I would not allow

Like a young sapling bending to the wind
And supple-proud not to snap in two

For what is wind that rips away bright leaves
But a hollow thief? And I so sure
Of new leavings come each Spring

Soft bark heeds not the heated sun of day
Nor the sharp claws of night

It grows, sheds, and rebirths in tune
With the melodies we call the seasons

But then one day comes murdering ice
Or heavy-fingered strangling wind

And the tree no longer bends but breaks
In weak and trembling age

So frail and rooted to destiny

Now must we break and snap
And crash to the ground

The muddied leaves like so many tears
Stored up for grieving this fated day.

Ylang-Ylang

My most vivid memory is fragrance:
Heavy clouds of jasmine
Like an iron pendant hanging
From the bright yellow flowers
But more—
An undertone of the bitter orange neroli
With just a tinkling of metallic
Savored on the tongue.

When deeply inhaled
There is the remembrance of custard
Of banana
Even of the rubber nipple of a baby's bottle.

So aroma and taste enfold
Into feeling
And in the mind's eye
Is the sharp scene of a dusty road
Where the ylang-ylang trees bow low
In the moonlight
And their flaxen blossoms
Throw their scent to the stars.

Yet this memory is not my own
But my father's
Of a tropical place far from here
Which I only imagine
When he closes his eyes and speaks of
Home.

Myrtles

The myrtles are running rampant
Going crazy like those women in
Nineteen seventy-two reading
The very first issue of Ms magazine
Discovering themselves.

The myrtles have banded together
To drop their crepe all over my yard
In riotous colors of purple red pink
And even the soft lilac
(Which is a tree of another trope)

As if it were a fête they were throwing
After the funeral of a beloved (ahem!) husband.

And now that the world has been recolored:
The shed roof a hot pink
Lawn a scarlet red
 Pampas grass whispering purple
And the bird bath swirling little lilac waves

The crepe myrtles straighten back up
Drained of their sensual blossoms
To stand tall and silent
Returned to their empty dignity
Of brown branch.

Fountain

My husband did not understand the significance of water,
So when he was alive we did not talk of fountains or renewal;
But soon after he died and I honored his life with a plaque,
I built a fountain in the backyard not far from him.

The jays and mourning doves drink heartily from it
Scooping with their beaks and tilting heavenward
To swallow the cool and transparent water.

Some tiny toadlets appear among the rocks:
Dark green shadows that hop behind the fountain's face
To nestle in the pebbled puddles of mud.
(I imagine them joyful reincarnations of honorable humans.)

On hot summer days the water tumbles out
Defiant against the brutal Texas sun,
Its splashing laughter echoing softly in the yard.

My husband's plaque still stands there
Accompanied by another honoring a son who died too early.
I am simply a watcher now,
No longer wife nor mother:
One who has learned that water soothes
And the sound of it diminishes grief.

Spirit

Shall I follow you down by the river under the leaf-full trees,
Or into the hidden garden past the jumbled rock homes of snakes,
Through the briar hedges that cling and claw and clutch my arms?
And all the while I wonder where you take me, will you break me
Like the helpless ocean that crashes on the barren, sandy shore?

I am the water that takes its shape from everything that touches me,
The vulnerable body upon whom the world may make its mark
Which dissipates in the cracks and crevices of rock on which I flow.
You think me weak because I choose surrender
Yet yielding is in itself the greater strength:
I wait, I scheme, I bide my solitary time.
In loneliness.

              Still you persist in pursuing me
Intruding on my dreams like an enduring worm of hunger
Whose appetite consumes each stray and sleeping thought
Until I wake in a nightmare dark of frightful chittering
From which I flee while peaceful dawn flows through the window.

Will nothing ever change? The seasons remain fixed in their place,
The clock cannot grow more numbers to mark its standard hours,
Day and night, dawn and dusk, all keep their time in combat unison.
So must I struggle to remember to forget you
To forget to remember you as I trail your shadow and cry:
"Through death you have abandoned me" but still I feel
The tendrils of your embrace that pull me closer.

Our Place

Earth is quiet, slumbering under the relentless sun
Whose anger dissipates into the dusty, crimson soil.
What lives below has fed on fallen flesh and bloodless bone
And knows its life will, in its turn, do quite the same.
What else do we live for
                    Except to nourish the future?

So if we put an ear to the ground, or go barefoot,
We might know the sound and feel of teeming life
Beneath us:
                    The scurry of colonies obeying their queen,
The writhing ecstasy of brainless worms
The slimy trail of blind slugs digging toward daylight.
What else can we do
                    Except applaud our discovery?

We congratulate ourselves for our cleverness,
Our striving to knowledge
                    Our gamut of emotions
But we forget
                    Except perhaps alone, in the dark,
That our pulsing hearts and hectic brains will one day feed
The ants, the worms, the slugs, and all the life
On earth, in earth, under sky, in sky, underneath and
overhead,
For we are simply fodder for the universe.

Waking

[from "Mist" by Kirk Wilson: *"I watched my father die and did not see the mist/ It could be a clouding of the mind that kept me from it."* quoted with permission of author.]

I wake early this morning to feed the restless cats,
Clean out their yesterday's-dinner dishes,
And I recall how much you loved these dawn-breaking hours:

The sky barely pink at the horizon
And stretching lazily to dispel the night
With all the pastels touched and warmed by the sun.

This was your time of day,
Puttering softly through the house,
Checking that locks were still locked,
Thankfully unaltered and secure from the day before
Because you were a keeper of routine,
Because you husbanded time,

As you did your summer vegetable garden every year,
Pulling out the unruly weeds,
Staking each plant into its rightful place,
Puffing your pipe to confuse the gnats,
And gently relocating each offending insect
From the tomatoes' fuzzy leaves.

Finally you slipped out to the silent yard,
To the seat that you had so carefully positioned to face the dawn,
And smoked your pipe and sighed and leaned back
To let the sun's soft hand caress away the chill on your cheek
And shine bright sparkles of light behind your eyes,

To confirm the quotidian dawn, the mundane magic
That was the secret of your serenity
Yet unknown to your careless daughter,
Who slept away these hours until she lost you
And has to make her own peace with each dawning day.

Between

Eye of the dove
eye of the hurricane

I fall into the space
between calm and chaos

Listening
and counting the heartbeats

Throbbing into my frantic brain
Signaling conflict:

Bird and cat fight for dominion
One by persistence
the other by terror.

(Are you afraid to be eaten
or that you will not eat?)

Water and wind struggling for dominance
One by engulfing
the other by flattening.

(Will we be drowned
or strangled?)

And in the vacuum between where soul is shredded,
Its torn fragments left unintelligible, we lay
Helpless
looking into the dark empty eye of the dove
the wild swirling eye of the hurricane.

What The Rain Brings

There is nothing so angry as pouring rain,
A manic preacher's fist beating evil
Out of a weary soul, shaking loose the early summer buds,
Drowning the last of late Spring's promise.

First the thunder calling from a distance,
Beckoning us submerged in dreams,
To break the bonds of sleep
That caress, arrest, in thoughtless slumber:

A fretless prison
In which carelessness reigns.

After, the lightning that sparks through the room
Like a single match ignited, giving way to
Almost-dawn. Then, living silence as quiet as
Unconscious breath before
The crash, the lashing rain.

And when the rain abates, creates
Its clean, pure, unsullied ground for planting,
We return from sleep to the world of care,
Despair.

September

September is the dead month
When summer kneels exhausted
And fall glides quietly forward
Dragging behind the cold specter
Of eternal silence.
It is our time of resignation
Recognizing in orange and brown
The crisp finality of this life
And in nature's undressing
The loss and emptying of our joy.

"A blue sky morning turned into
The blackest of nights," he said.
When broadcasts could not fill the dead space
All we heard was the thud of desperate bodies
Wanting to fly from the searing heat.
Remember the billowing smoky silence
After the towers fell inward
Their mortar mumbling into disintegration
While trapped saviors fell mute with surprise.
Our tears of sorrow, rage, revenge
Would not dispel the ash-filled air.

You left me quietly while I nodded off
Unable to maintain my vigil in faith;
You had cried for your mother
And had fought your son who wanted only
To embrace and comfort you.
But you kept the last insult for me:
To slip away silently
Without words of love or assurance
So I would wonder: What was your last thought?

This is a time without renewal
When all goes to ground
To underground
To the dark hush of sleeping roots.
Here is not hibernation but decay,
Our voices strangled and parched;
The snows to come cannot reach
So deep to nourish us.

Cardinals

Every morning and evening the cardinals
Come to stock up their nest, to
Feed their young, I suppose.

They do not know stillness or
The silence of emptiness, twittering
From branch to ground to branch
While their hearts beat wildly
With unexamined life.

Am I to envy them, be
Jealous of their vacuum of emotion,
Covet what they lack?

I struggle with vacancy:
Seeing them
Remembering my speeding heartbeat
Gripped heavily now
In the consciousness of loss.

In The Luxembourg Gardens

I am willing to admit that my own retrospect is touched by a sentimental sunset, the memory of a friend coming across the Luxembourg Gardens in the late afternoon, waving a branch of lilac, a friend who was later (so far as I could find out) to be mixed with the mud of Gallipoli. (T.S. Eliot, "A Commentary" *The Criterion* April 1934)

You watch him
As he strides toward you
In the fresh, wet evening,
His smile broadening as he approaches,
And the lilac branch in his hand thick with purple.

You straighten, and
Shift from foot to foot,
Your heels sinking into the rain-soaked grass.
The green sparkles with silver droplets.

You eagerly greet him with a sturdy embrace
And an innocent, inviting smile of welcome and relief
That celebrates the pale blue sky
And the shimmering marble fountain.

He has returned to you as he said he would
And laughed at your unease, left
Alone at this end of the Gardens
In its riot of sunset.

After all, you are simply
A young student
Intoxicated with Paris,
Yet afraid of it all.

You will accompany him back
To the rooms at Rue Saint Jacques,
His arm careless across your shoulders,
Your steps keeping tempo with his stride.

And you will climb the stairs,
Drink wine from simple crazed tumblers,
Put the flowering branch in a glass of water,
And read poetry to one another

Until it is too dark to see, and
All that you will keep in your heart is
The scent of lilacs.

Nature's Lesson

Who faults the flytrap for seducing the fly
Throbbing its ruby lips in a promising kiss?
Or the yellow pitcher trumpeting its music
To curl in sugar the unwary butterfly?

How can the docile shrimp resist the simulated worm
Dangling just above the hungry mouth
The hairy frogfish sensuously wiggles to entice?

Or the mollusk withstand the lithesome dance
Of the doe-eyed saber-toothed blenny
Whose jagged teeth will rip away chunks of unwary flesh?

What blame or censure, then,
When the one with tender hands
And whispering kisses
Lures you to an embrace
That devours your love?

Careless

Does the rose bush remember what it should do
Each spring to breathe and grow again?
It should sharpen its thorns to adamantine edges
To keep away the hungry aphids
Seeking buds and burgeoning leaves.
It should turn its propagating gently to the sun
And bathe itself in morning dew
Drinking cloudy nectar.

Does the moth remember what it should do
In summer to dance itself in joy?
It should flutter its powdered wings like glitter
Absorbed from distant stars
To discourage the dark spider in its somber web
From the temptation of tasty
Gossamer and furry flesh.
It should fly high in the sun baked leaves of trees
To nourish its larva and cocoon.

Does the woman remember what she should do
While folded in the arms of a lover?
She should revel in the warmth and comfort
And keep in mind each soft, endearing word
To ease the grief of future loss and
Inevitable separation.

There in the world:
The rose will fade, wither, and die
Its petals decay into paper
Blown away by the wind.
The moth will weaken and totter
Into an irresistible flame one night
To be consumed into blackened ashes.
The woman will walk away
Mindless of her weakness
To not have loved enough.

When

It is time now: the caterpillar, duckling, tadpole, nymph
Must all extend, distend, and broaden
Soft bones bend and rearrange
Limbs untangle and alter for the transformation.

One face must melt into another
Each feature change by clear design
Of innate, unyielding dispositions
Required by nature's strict regulations.

A seed becomes a leaf
A leaf becomes a branch
The branch thickens to a tree
By the temperament of time.

There is no discussion nor argument
To change the immutable:
Time and environment always prevail.

So with our grief that now disposes
Its sad and heavy coat,
Now sheds its weary darkness.
It, too, transforms to drop its familiar trappings
And emerge in sunlight as remembrance.

From chrysalis emerges memory,
Sorrow now scraped away
And the newborn awash with blissful rain.

Permanence

The bloom of the hydrangea may be more breathtaking
And lush in its multiple fullness,

The peaches more fragrant and heavy
As they drag the branch down toward the dark, moist earth;

The jays and doves come with ruffled wings,
Only recently awakened from shells, with unsteady gait,

And the butterflies need multiple attempts
Before they can sip enough nectar
And flutter off with footprints of pollen.

All these tell nature's transient story.

There is a richer tale hidden deep in the unseen germinating seed,
In the fruit's ovarian pit that harbors life,
In the fragile eggs coddled and warmed in tree-blind nests,

And in the sticky-webbed cocoons where
Ugly, prickly-haired caterpillars dream of beauty.

We are allowed only a moment's glance
Before all goes underground
To a restless sleep
Anticipating another dawn.

Orchid

The orchid is so fragile but demanding:
No direct light, not too much water,
A great deal of compliment
To give it confidence
And it dies anyway
Dramatically:

Edges of petals brown as if
Burned with passion
Then dropping with a whisper
To lay still in tangled roots
And hard, glass-shiny leaves.

I bring it weekly to the sink
Like leading a caravan to the oasis
Deluge it with cool water
Then watch and wait
As it sheds the liquid like molting feathers
To the whisperings of twisted tendrils—
The end of thirst.

Until I can carry it back
To the sarabande of touch
And the fragrance bursts forth
Like the soprano's coloratura.

What Is Not There

It is still there just below the surface
Under the sand under the rocks under the sea
Under the infinite sky

What the mourning dove cries to the sun and clouds
What the honeysuckle clings to for strength and scent
What each green and yearning thing in the garden wants

Human life ends at this threshold
Its words no match for the unspoken
Its muscles feeble compared to the branch

Here is silence and power
Potency of the natural world
Beyond me

I am mute and blind and deaf
I am numb and cold
Marked by the fire of regret

What should I have said?
Or saw? Or heard?
What should I have felt
To enclose and protect you?

Too late.
Now I note only the empty spaces
The unresponsive air
The heavy shadows
And the door that is forever closed.

Sandra Salinas Newton is a Filipina-American Professor Emeritus of English. Her published works include textbooks and a short story. Her poetry (more than sixty poems) has appeared in *OPEN: Journal of Arts and Letters and Vita Brevis Press, The Woolf, Vultures & Doves: Social Issues of Our Time, published by Valiant Scribe Literary Journal, Fauxmoir, The Ekphrastic Review, Apricity, Nothing Divine Dies, The Poetry of Nature of Vita Brevis Press, Neologism Poetry, The Decadent Review Provenance Journal, New Note Poetry, Oberon Poetry Journal 2021, Cerasus Magazine, Native Skin, and The Evening Street Press, Multiplicity, Etched Onyx, Midwest Quarterly, The Ponder Review* and *The Connecticut River Review*, among others. She was recently one of four finalists in the 2022 Writers' League of Texas Manuscript Contest (Historical Fiction category). She recently published three novels: *Born Again, A Passion For Tom*, and *Inevitable*. She earned her B.A. from The City College of New York, her M.A. from Hunter College, and her Ph.D. from Fordham University.

www.ingramcontent.com/pod-product-compliance
Lightning Source LLC
Chambersburg PA
CBHW022050080426

42734CB00009B/1291